THE G.I. SERIES

General John J. Pershing awards the Distinguished Service Cross to Private J. Parent of the 26th 'Yankee Division'. Parent wears the M1917 overcoat (distinguished by the cuff strap) with the 'YD' patch of his division and one overseas stripe indicating six months of overseas service. On his back he carries a full M-1910 haversack with the extended pack carrier strapped to the bottom. (26th Div. 2/19) NA

THE G. I. SERIES

THE ILLUSTRATED HISTORY OF THE AMERICAN SOLDIER, HIS UNIFORM AND HIS EQUIPMENT

Over There!
The American Soldier in World War I

Jonathan Gawne

CHELSEA HOUSE PUBLISHERS
PHILADELPHIA

First Chelsea House hardback edition published 2000.

©Lionel Leventhal Limited, 1997

Library of Congress Cataloging-in-Publication Data
Gawne, Jonathan.
Over there!: the American soldier in World War I / Jonathan Gawne.
   p.   cm.—(The G.I. series)
Originally published: London : Greenhill Books: Mechanicsburg, Pa., USA : Stackpole Books, © 1997.
Includes index
Summary: Describes the training, uniforms, equipment, and role of American soldiers fighting in Europe during World War I.
ISBN 0-7910-5371-7 (hc)
1. United States. Army—History—World War, 1914–1918 Pictorial works Juvenile literature.
2. United States. Army—Equipment Pictorial works Juvenile literature.   3. United States. Army—Supplies and stores Pictorial works Juvenile literature.   4. United States. Army—Uniforms Pictorial works Juvenile literature.   [1. United States. Army—History—World War, 1914–1918.   2. World War, 1914–1918.]   I. Title.
II. Series: G.I. series (Philadelphia, Pa.)
D570.2.G3   1999
940,4'1273'0222—dc21   99-22458
                                    CIP

DEDICATION

This book is dedicated to the memory of the men of the 3rd Corps Artillery Park. Far too few returned.

ACKNOWLEDGEMENTS

Thanks to all the individuals and institutions noted below who supplied photographs. The author would also like to make special mention of the staff of the Army Art Activity in the Center for Military History. Also to Jerry Jerner, Pete Tuttle, J. J. Jones, Jean-Pierre Verney, and the folks at Great War Militaria in Chambersburg, PA, for help and access to their collections. In order to assist readers in the use of this book, information on unit and month/year (when known) has been added at the end of each caption.

ABBREVIATIONS

AA	Army Art Activity, Center for Military History
JG	Jonathan Gawne
GG	George Ghastly
GWM	Great War Militaria
HM	Henry MacLure
JL	John Langellier
NA	National Archives
SK	Scott Kraska

Designed and edited by DAG Publications Ltd
Designed by David Gibbons
Layout by Anthony A. Evans
Printed in Hong Kong

OVER THERE!
THE AMERICAN SOLDIER
IN WORLD WAR I

If there was a miracle in the First World War, it was that the United States could take a tiny army of 200,000 men and expand it to a force of four million men (two million in France) within only nineteen months. By the end of the war the Americans had more men fighting in France than the British did. The American Army was not only fighting in France, but in Italy, Siberia and northern Russia. Entire industries that did not exist when America entered the war on 6 April 1917 had been rapidly developed and were in full production by the Armistice of 11 November 1918.

Although the war began for Europeans in 1914, America took little notice of it. Many immigrants returned home to fight for their former countries. A few Americans sought adventure and either joined the ranks of a friendly army or volunteered for hospital or ambulance work. The most famous volunteer group was the American Field Service which supplied ambulances and drivers to the French and British Armies. Over 32,000 Americans enlisted in the British Army, and many more joined the Canadian and French forces.

The pre-war American Army was composed of a scattered handful of small regiments, and a state-controlled militia known as the National Guard. In 1916 the U.S. Army was sent south to deal with Mexican revolutionaries who were raiding across the border. The regular army was strengthened by a few National Guard units that welcomed the experience and the excitement of mobilization. It was in Mexico that General John J. Pershing first made his mark. When America finally declared war on Germany in 1917, Pershing was given command of the American Expeditionary Force (AEF), the American military force sent to fight overseas.

America was in poor shape for a world war. It had few modern weapons and transport ships. National Guard units were called into Federal service and, along with the few regular army regiments, were fleshed out by draftees and volunteers into infantry divisions. These U.S. divisions were more than twice the size of French or British divisions. The greatest difficulty in sending the AEF to France was a shortage of transport space across the Atlantic. The solution to this shipping dilemma proved to be German passenger liners that had been commandeered by the Americans as spoils of war. The Allies (the British and French) agreed to furnish military equipment to the Americans in exchange for raw materials and a rapid deployment of American combat units.

The Allies wanted only American combat troops (infantry and machine gunners) to be sent over to fill out their depleted ranks. Pershing constantly had to argue against Americans being used in any formation smaller than a division. His aim was to form an independent American army, as well as the logistics and support troops needed to keep such an army in fighting shape. The rear area logistics were handled by the Service of Supply (SOS). To the dismay of the Allies, many of the 700,000 men of the SOS had to be assembled in France before the majority of the combat divisions could be brought over.

The typical soldier of 1917 was issued with olive drab wool breeches and tunic. His wool shirt was cut only halfway down the front. The generals felt that given a chance the men would wear their shirts fully unbuttoned, and that would present an unmilitary appearance. He wore canvas leggings, web ammo belt and pack, and a wide-brimmed campaign hat with a colored cord denoting his branch of service. In his M1910 pack he carried a wool blanket, half of a two-man pup tent, a wool overcoat, a mess tin, rations, toiletry equipment, and spare shirt, socks and underwear. Most of the troops were trained as expert riflemen, but had never seen a machine gun, grenade or modern artillery piece.

When the divisions were ready to be shipped overseas, the troops were issued two gas masks: the lightweight French M2 for use with weak gas and smoke, and the British-designed small box respirator for the more powerful poison gases. It would not be until January 1918 that the American-built version of the British mask went into production. The men also received the British flat steel helmet. Since the men were to wear the helmet in combat, they had no way to carry their beloved campaign hats. So these hats were taken away (to be cut up into felt slippers for casualties) and replaced by a simple wool overseas cap. The canvas leggings were also replaced by spirally wrapped wool puttees.

The M1903 Springfield rifle was the most accurate infantry weapon in the world. Unfortunately there were not enough production facilities to make them for all the troops. The majority of American soldiers received the M1917 Enfield, based on the British Pattern 14 rifle. The first twelve divisions to land in France were issued the French Chauchat automatic rifle as their light machine gun, and the French Hotchkiss as their heavy machine gun. The next eleven divisions sent overseas were given the British Vickers machine gun in place of the Hotchkiss (along with the Chauchat). After July 1917, the remaining divisions were issued with the American-built Browning Automatic Rifle and Browning M1917 machine gun.

The primary combat unit was the fifty-nine-man infantry platoon composed of a six-man headquarters, a seventeen-man rifle section, a nine-man rifle grenadier section, a twelve-man hand grenade section, and a fifteen-man automatic rifle section with two Chauchats. Four platoons made up an infantry company, and four companies made up a 1,027-man battalion. Three battalions, along with a machine-gun company, supply and headquarters section made up a regiment. Two infantry regiments and a machine-gun battalion made a brigade. The 28,000-man division was composed of two infantry brigades, one artillery brigade (comprising two light and one heavy artillery regiment, and a trench mortar battery), an engineer regiment, a machine-gun battalion and a signal battalion.

The Americans were so short of trained manpower that the 2nd Division was composed of two Army regiments and two U.S. Marine Corps regiments. These marines went to France in their forest-green colored uniforms. Pershing, claiming it was difficult to supply them with a special uniform, ordered them to change into standard army olive drab. To show their identity they added Marine Corps collar disks to their new Army tunics, and fixed their traditional eagle, globe and anchor insignia to the front of their helmets.

Almost all of the artillery used by the Americans was French-built. The two light artillery regiments in a division were composed of twenty-four of the rapid-firing French 75mm guns. The single heavy artillery regiment in a division had twenty-four of the French 155mm Schneider howitzers. The trench mortar units used either the British 3- or 6-inch Stokes mortar. The Allies also supplied almost all the aeroplanes used by the Americans. Not one American-built combat plane would fight in the war. Only a handful of American-built observation craft were sent to Europe. The French two-man Renault tank was supplied to the American light tank units, and the British Mark V tank was given to the heavy tank battalions.

As more and more Yanks were shipped to France, newspaper correspondents decided they needed a nickname for the common American soldier (such as 'Tommy' for the British or 'Poilu' for the French). One suggestion was 'Sammy', after Uncle Sam. This name, although popular with the French, was universally hated by the Americans. Eventually the name 'Doughboy', which previously was reserved only for infantrymen, came to stand for any American soldier. The term doughboy is thought to have come from the Mexican Border Expedition and the Spanish word for the local sun-dried brick, 'adobe'. Cavalrymen had taken to calling the marching, dust-covered infantrymen 'adobes', which eventually turned into 'doughboys'.

General Pershing refused to permit the units of the AEF to be broken up and given to other armies piecemeal. He allowed his men to be trained by the Allies, then serve brief periods under their command to accustom them to combat. His plan to bring all the units of the AEF together under a specific American Army had to be altered when the Russian Army collapsed on the Eastern Front. This allowed Germany to transfer a number of new divisions to France. In March 1918 these fresh German divisions overwhelmed the French and British lines in a desperate attempt to end the war. The Allies asked for immediate help from the Americans, and Pershing agreed to use his troops wherever they would do the most good.

On 28 May 1918 elements of the 1st Division (which had been the first to land in France, and would be the last to leave after the war) became the first American troops to go into action under direct American command. They took and held the small town of Cantigny against three counterattacks, thus proving that the Americans could fight. The Marine Brigade, part of the 2nd Division, took the heavily defended woods at Belleau and provided a needed boost to Allied morale. At the Marne the 3rd Division held against strong German attacks, and from that point on the Germans were forced back onto the defensive. With the SOS in place to provide a foundation for the American Army, more divisions poured in from across the Atlantic as the British Navy began transporting American troops. At one point 10,000 American soldiers were landing in France every day.

The doughboys learned to prevent trenchfoot by changing their socks regularly in cold, wet weather. They also learned to hate the 'cootie' or body lice. In one report it was estimated that over 90 per cent of all men at the front line were infested with these small insects that constantly irritated their hosts and transmitted disease. New soldiers soon learned to pass the seams of their uniforms over candle flames to kill any 'cootie' eggs.

A number of small changes to the American uniform had occurred since America entered the war. To ensure that officers of all the Allied nations received proper treatment and respect from all enlisted men (who might not recognize the different rank insignia of various nations), American officers were required to wear a leather belt and cross strap known as a Sam Browne belt. Small chevrons were sewn to the right sleeve of any soldier who had suffered a wound, and similar chevrons were sewn to the left sleeve to indicate each period of six months' service overseas.

The most significant addition to the uniform was the authorization of shoulder-sleeve insignia indicating the unit to which the soldier was attached. The 81st Division started this trend unofficially, and late in the war Pershing authorized all major commands to design their own shoulder patch. For most units these patches would not be made or worn until the fighting had ended, and in most cases not until the men actually returned to the United States.

Although the American Army had successfully used Negro troops to fight in the Indian Wars, the senior commanders were convinced that Negroes should only be used in stevedore and labor units. Two divisions, the 92nd and 93rd, were composed of Negro enlisted men and white officers. These divisions were given to the French, who armed and equipped them for combat. Both units performed well under fire, although back home they never received the recognition they deserved.

Italy had been asking for American units to help it fight against the Austrian Army. In July 1918 the 332nd Regiment was sent to Italy to help bolster the line. Six American divisions were lent to the British Army in northern France during the final year of the war. These divisions amounted to more than twelve full-strength British divisions. To simplify supplying these men, many were armed with British weapons and issued British rations and supplies.

The situation in Russia had become very confused in 1918. The revolution had overthrown the Tsar, but many different factions were fighting for control of the vast country. The Allies were worried that the massive stocks of military supplies they had sent to the Tsar would be captured by either the Germans or the Bolsheviks, so they sent small expeditions to both northern Russia and Siberia. These multi-national forces fought in terrible winter conditions. The last American troops did not leave Russia until April 1920.

On 12 September 1918 the Allies went over to the offensive, and the American 1st Army captured the German-held salient at St Mihiel in heavy fighting. This success was followed up with a continued attack into the thickly defended

Meuse–Argonne area. The attacks continued against the German lines until 1 November when the main German defenses were shattered. On 6 November the Germans requested a cease-fire.

At 11 a.m. on 11 November the Armistice (cease-fire) went into effect. The German Army retreated into its own country and the fighting came to an end. In case a peace treaty could not be negotiated, the Allies insisted they be allowed to take up new positions inside Germany. This led to the creation of the new American Third Army, to be known as the Army of Occupation. The Third Army served in occupied Germany until 1923.

The final insignia added to the doughboy's uniform was a red chevron sewn halfway down the left arm. This was the discharge stripe, indicating that the soldier had served honorably in the war, and had been returned to civilian life.

One important aspect of the war that is often overlooked is the influenza epidemic of 1918. An outbreak of a deadly form of 'flu' struck all over the world. Germany, with food supplies cut back by an Allied naval blockade, was particularly hard hit. This epidemic ended up killing more American doughboys than were actually killed in combat. Many soldiers returned safely home, only to fall ill and die in a military hospital.

As soon as the war ended, the German military circulated a rumor that they had been stabbed in the back by the civilian government, and had not been defeated in the field. Nothing could have been further from the truth. In the final days of fighting, the German Army was worn out and short of all types of supplies. More importantly, the German defensive lines had been overwhelmed by the Allies. Individual German soldiers may still have been able to fight, but the country was no longer able to defend itself against a large-scale offensive.

The actual contribution of the United States to the First World War has always been debated. Some claim that the Americans entered the war too late to have any real impact. The fact is that the Allied armies were crumbling under the 1918 German offensive. The Germans even admitted they had to make a desperate effort to end the war before the Americans got their troops to France. At the time everyone knew that the Allied lines had only held because of the Americans. This does not in any way demean the other Allied armies; it is just that the Americans were there at the right time when they were most needed. Had the doughboys not been in France, or not been skilled fighters, the outcome of the war might have been very different.

The U.S. Army had wanted to develop a new uniform at the end of the war, but there was an enormous number of surplus uniforms that needed to be used up first. In 1926 the first major uniform change occurred when the old-style closed collar tunic was changed to an open collar tunic worn with shirt and tie. This new open collar tunic would be worn right up to the Second World War. By the time fighting ended, the wool breeches had been replaced with straight-leg wool trousers, but the peacetime Army reverted to the traditional military-style breeches until they were finally eliminated in 1938.

A footnote of the AEF occurred in July 1932 when veterans of the war, suffering from the effects of the Great Depression, marched on Washington asking for an early payment of a bonus the government had voted to award them. They called themselves the Bonus Expeditionary Force, or BEF. Although the marchers were peaceful and the President did not want any violence, Army Chief of Staff Douglas MacArthur ordered American troops and tanks to push out the civilians. Only a few were killed, but it was a sad conclusion for the men who had fought the war to end all wars.

FOR FURTHER READING

The Doughboys, Lawrence Stallings, Harper and Row, 1963.

Make the Kaiser Dance, Henry Berry, Doubleday & Co., 1978.

Into the Breach – American Women Overseas in WWI, Dorothy and Carl Schneider, Viking Books, 1991.

Treat 'em Rough – The Birth of American Armor, Dale Wilson, Presidio Press, 1989.

The U.S. Air Service in the Great War, 1917-1919, James Cooke, Praeger, 1996.

World War One Collectors Handbook, Otoupalik and Gordon, 1977.

Left: John J. Pershing led the American Expeditionary Force (AEF) from conception, through combat, to victory. The Distinguished Service Cross ribbon is seen over his left pocket. Although he had refused the DSC for service in WW1, President Roosevelt awarded it to him on his eightieth birthday for his heroic actions against the Moro tribesmen in the Philippines. He is seen here wearing the four stars of a General of the Armies: the first man ever to hold that rank in the American Military. AA

Below: The U.S. Army moved from blue to olive drab uniforms from 1910 to 1912. These dress blue uniforms were kept on as a reminder of the traditional use of 'army blue'. In the war years the 'dress blues' were relegated to special functions – primarily at the White House. A special effort was made to discourage new officers from buying dress blue uniforms, to take some of the strain off the overworked garment industry. JL

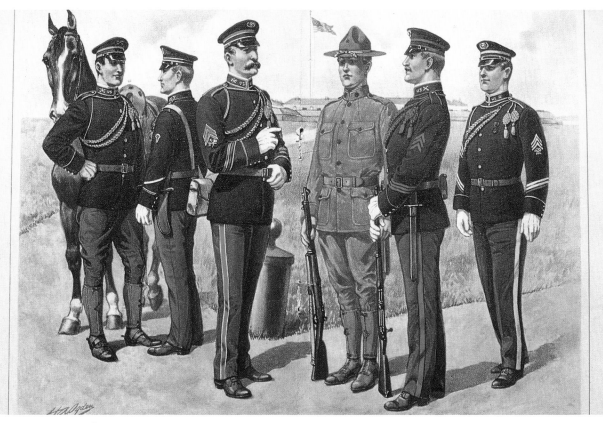

Left: These typical AEF uniforms show a man with full pack at left, a soldier with overseas cap and M2 gas mask and box respirator at the carry position, a soldier with steel helmet and gas mask bag at the ready position, and a general (note braid on sleeves) in short wool overcoat, leather puttees and service hat. AA

Left: This group of photographers, carrying the rounded M2 gas mask bag, are being observed by an officer in his trench coat and gas mask at the ready (left). Behind them are a group of French enlisted men in their horizon blue uniforms and overseas hats. These hats were copied by the Americans as a replacement for the bulky campaign hat. AA

Right: This group of signalers form part of an artillery unit, as denoted by the red cord on their campaign hats. In the background a 75mm gun is seen in action. At left an officer in wool shirt and black tie displays the gold and black hat cord worn by all U.S. Army officers. The enlisted men wear both leather and canvas leggings, which indicates that this scene is located either in the United States or well behind the front lines. For comfort they wear their shirt collar out over the rough collar of their tunics. AA

Right: This officer wears the standard wool uniform with 'U.S.' and branch insignia on both sides of the collar. The service cap has light brown braid around the sides to indicate an officer's cap. The brown leather belt with cross strap was known as a 'Sam Browne' belt, and was required for all Allied officers in Europe. The belt indicated to all enlisted men that the wearer was an officer, even if they had no idea of his nationality or rank. NA

W.S.S.
WAR SAVINGS STAMPS
ISSUED BY THE
UNITED STATES
GOVERNMENT

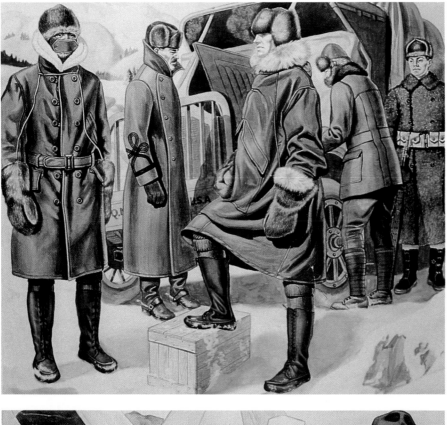

Left: The North Russian Expeditionary Force wore a variety of warm uniforms. From left to right are an overcoat with sheepskin lining, a major in his officer's wool overcoat, an early parka, a mechanic with a short driver's coat and a soldier in the British-issue mohair overcoat. Most of the men wear various forms of fur or lambskin mittens and hats. Boots would either be heavily greased leather boots, or Arctic overshoes. AA

Left: This plate displays some of the uniforms worn by women who have enrolled for war work and are being trained in a military-style camp. Although not official military uniforms, note how the styling gets as close as possible to 'regulation' military appearance. For practical purposes the long skirts have been shortened, thus initiating a fashion trend that would keep skirt lengths shrinking for long after the fighting. AA

Right: These female Red Cross workers display some of the different types of uniforms worn by that service. At left is the red-lined cape of a nurse. Officially, the Red Cross was to handle relief work, while the YMCA was to provide for amusement and recreation of the troops. AA

Right: These 1941 versions of the standard infantry uniforms are essentially what the troops wore for most of the 1930s. The over-coat at left, and wool coat (third from left) were the two principal uniforms of the post-1926 G.I. The M1941 field jacket (second from left) started the trend toward more utilitarian military garments. At right is an officer in his short wool overcoat and 'pink' breeches. Headgear during the 1930s would be either the campaign hat, or the 1917 A1 helmet – essentially the same as the WW1 helmet but with a different liner and a web chin-strap. AA

Left: The different colors of American uniforms can be seen in these unissued examples. Although variations did occur, these specimens were chosen as being the most representative. From top to bottom: Marine Corps forest-green wool with red discharge stripe, olive drab cotton fatigue, blue denim cotton fatigue, M1911 olive drab cotton uniform, M1917 olive drab wool, M1912 wool with North Russian Expeditionary patch, officer's wool uniform with 332nd Regiment patch. GWM

Right: Only a few units painted insignia on their steel helmets before the end of the war, but as soon as the fighting stopped it became a fad. These three examples represent the major types of painted helmets commonly found. Left: A U.S. Marine Corps helmet with the eagle, globe and anchor insignia fastened over the 2nd Division Indian-head insignia. The yellow square indicates that this helmet is from the 1st Battalion – 6th Marine Regiment. Bottom is a 'diary' helmet with information about the owner's travels through the war, with the insignia of the 79th Division on the front. Top is a camouflage pattern which was rarely (if at all) used by doughboys in combat. GWM

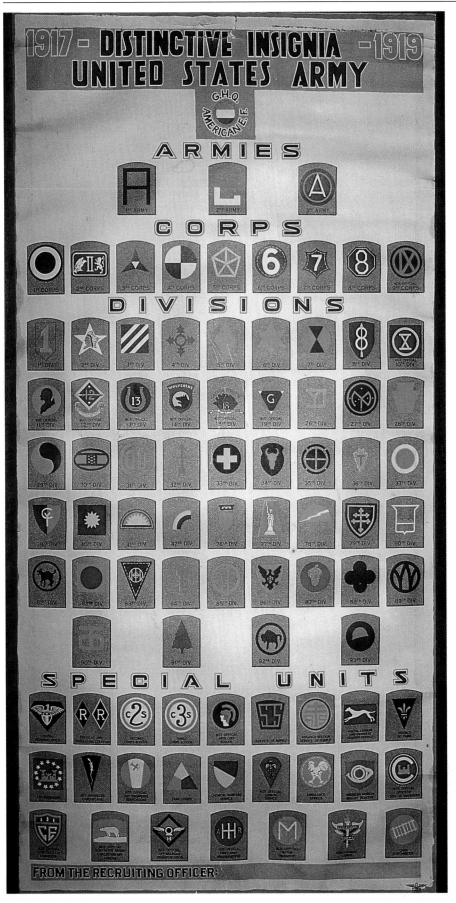

Left: This post-war recruiting poster shows many of the shoulder sleeve designs developed at the end of the war. The majority of these insignia were never worn during combat, and some were not made until long after the war was over: most were added to uniforms by veterans after they had returned home. GWM

Below: This corporal wears the standard uniform in which the AEF went to war: the Model 1917 wool tunic, wool breeches, spiral puttees and the Montana peak campaign hat. The cord around this hat was colored in the soldier's branch of service (light blue for infantry, red for artillery, etc). Officers of all branches wore a gold and black hat cord. JG

Above: This signalman wears the summer uniform of olive drab cotton tunic and breeches. It is commonly referred to as the M-1910 uniform, since that is the year that the Army changed from khaki to olive drab colored cotton. In reality this design of tunic was not adopted until 1911. Only a handful of cotton uniforms were shipped to Europe and they rarely saw use in France. (8/18) NA

Above left: The first American units to serve overseas were volunteer medical groups such as these men from the Dartmouth College Medical School. Such units were unable to wear the American uniform because their country was not yet officially at war, so they adopted versions of either the French or British uniform with their own insignia. They staffed hospitals, thus taking the strain off the overworked French and British medical service. NA

Above right: Stanley Wadsworth Birch was one of many students who left Harvard University to drive an ambulance for the American Field Service. He is seen here in the British-pattern AFS uniform, complete with the special driver's cap bearing 184th Sanitary Unit markings. Many of these drivers were killed or wounded by artillery shelling while bringing casualties to the rear. The AFS became the stylish organization for young college men, eager for adventure, to join in the years before America entered the war. SK

Above: Most of the volunteer ambulance services used converted Ford Model T cars such as these of Ambulance Section 22. The Model T proved remarkably resilient and its light weight allowed it to travel on poor roads very close to the front lines. A devout pacifist, Henry Ford refused to sell his cars to the Ambulance Service at anything less than full retail price, as he did not want to promote militarism in any way. NA

Right: Lieutenant Walter Rheno volunteered for the French Air Force as a fighter pilot in 1916 and served in the Lafayette Escadrille (the Lafayette Squadron). This unit of American airmen transferred to the American Army in late 1917 and became the U.S. 103rd Aero Squadron. He wears a French aviator's uniform complete with the French pilot's round wing. The French cap seen here would later be copied by the Americans for their overseas cap. HM

Above: The New York State Militia's 'Fighting 69th' Regiment bids a fond farewell before leaving for federal service. The New York 69th would be renamed the 165th U.S. Regiment and be made part of the 42nd 'Rainbow' Division in the United States Army. The men wear the campaign, or Montana peak hat, along with different models of canvas leggings. (42nd Div. 8/17) NA

Opposite page, top: In the 1916 expedition to Mexico, the cavalry was the main force of the U.S. Army. In Europe only a handful of cavalrymen would see any action, and for the first time the horsemen would take a back seat to the infantry. This trooper wears the cavalry equipment standard in October 1918. A Springfield rifle is in the scabbard on the horse's left side. (10/18) JG

Opposite page bottom: Until the National Guard was called out for the Mexican Expedition it had obsolete equipment and acted more as a social club. The units that saw service on the Mexican border received valuable training and experience that allowed them to be sent to France rapidly when war was declared. These men of an unknown National Guard unit are armed with the 1903 Springfield rifle and wear the 1905 ammo belt with a variety of private purchase and militia uniform items. (JG)

ROCK ISLAND AF

183-31153   0
Cavalryman: equipe

Ⓐ /3449

Above: Officers pose in Brest, France, after disembarking from transport ships. The doctor at center wears the officer's model of the medical belt. These pouches contained surgical equipment and drugs. Both his companions carry dispatch (map) cases. The chaplain on the right carries the regulation two-snap first-aid pouch that contained one large bandage. Note the two sailors in the background with the two different styles of U.S. Navy hats. (61st Inf. Regt. 5/18) NA

Opposite page, top: Color bearers of the 16th Infantry Regiment prepare for the first U.S. parade through Paris to show the French that the Yanks have arrived. The campaign hats would pose a problem when the troops were issued with steel helmets, as there was no practical way to carry these felt hats in a pack. The campaign hats would be used to make felt slippers for casualties, and the men given wool 'overseas caps' instead. (1st Div. 7/17) NA

Right: Engineers building a camp in France wait for food with their mess kits. They wear a mixture of army sweaters and fatigue (work) clothing. Before the war the denim fatigue clothing was olive drab in color, but a shortage of material and dye prompted the use of blue denim instead. The blue fatigues would continue to be used up to the start of World War II. Most of the men also wear the wide-brimmed cotton fatigue hat. NA

Left: A chaplain with the 316th Infantry Regiment wears the issue raincoat with its metal buckles. He carries his gas mask bag at the slung position. The horizontal ridges showing through the left side of the bag are ridges along the gas mask canister inside. Air was drawn through the material in the canister to filter out the gas. These ridges kept the air from traveling unfiltered up the smooth side of the canister. (79th Div. 11/18)

Below: The idea of a wool-lined leather jerkin was borrowed from the British Army. This warm garment allowed much greater freedom of movement than an overcoat. The wool overseas cap replaced the campaign hat soon after the Americans arrived in France. The overseas cap could be folded flat and easily stored when the soldier was wearing his helmet, then taken out and worn in a non-combat area. (11/18) NA

Right: Officers at the front lines were issued enlisted men's uniforms to wear in combat. This 2nd lieutenant wears a rough wool M1918 tunic (note the lack of a patch pocket). The Sam Browne leather belt was regulation for all officers of every Allied country in Europe. His overseas cap, unlike the plain enlisted hat, has a piping in the color of his branch of service: a reminder of the old campaign hat cord. (5th Div. 12/18) NA

Left: Lieutenant Colonel Donovan of the 165th Infantry Regiment (former 69th New York) wears ribbons for a Distinguished Service Cross and a French Croix de Guerre. Most officer's uniforms were tailor-made; thus many small variations can be found in the material or pattern. On each side of his collar he wears national insignia (U.S.) and branch insignia (crossed rifles of infantry). Donovan, who would later run the OSS in WW2, wears a cloth cover over his steel helmet. (42nd Div. 9/18) NA

Left: Wearing the trenchcoat at left is the U.S. Secretary of War, Newton Baker. With him is a hometown neighbor. This marine is wearing the forest-green Marine Corps uniform which can be identified by the pleated pockets, twin seams on the chest, and turnback cuff that comes to a point. The marine's cross straps are for the small box respirator and the smaller M2 French gas mask. (2nd Div. 3/18) NA

Above right: This group of military policemen from the 1st MP Company wear the MP armband with solid letters. The small bags are for the French M2 gas mask. Their overseas caps with high peak and curved front are of French manufacture. The sergeant wears a sharpshooter medal. Most regulars took great pride in their marksmanship because those who wore these medals got extra pay. (1st Div. 3/18) NA

Below: A chaplain (center) with Sam Browne belt supervises the burial of American casualties. The man second from right has his dog tags exposed. The one square tag was a field expedient used when the order was issued for all men to wear a second tag in August 1917. Not enough round tags were available, so the Army authorized square tags as a temporary replacement. If the man was killed, one tag would stay with the body, the other would be sent to headquarters as proof of his death. (1st Div. 7/18) NA

Above: By the entrance to a dugout behind the lines, a soldier tries to pick 'cooties' (lice) out of his shirt. The other men wear their gas masks at the 'alert' position ready for instant use. The standing figure at left wears a British tunic, as identified by the collar and pleated pocket. The extreme shortage of American uniforms early in the war caused large numbers of British tunics and trousers to be issued to American soldiers. (42nd Div. 7/18) NA

Below: In a demonstration of how to use the M1910 haversack, the sergeant is placing two tins of hard bread into the top section of the pack along with spare clothes and small personal items. He will then fold up the pack around these items and attach the roll (composed of the blanket and tent) to the bottom. In order to take anything out of the top section of the pack, the entire assembly had to be taken apart. (2/19) NA

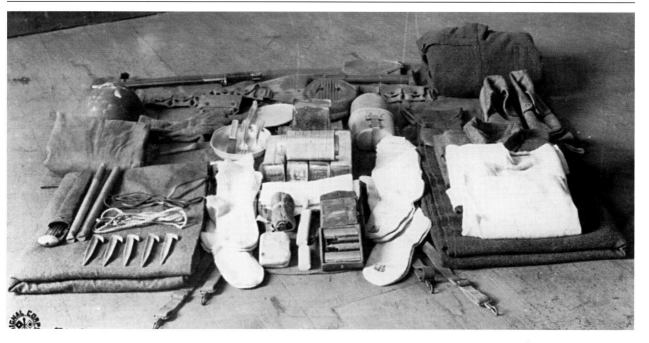

Above: The contents of the pack used in heavy marching order is displayed. This includes the pup tent on the left and spare clothing on the right. In the center the double-ended condiment can rests on four sealed metal cans of hard bread. Emergency food had to be sealed in metal to prevent contamination by poison gas in the front lines. (2/19) NA

Below: An eight-man squad in heavy marching order, which includes the overcoat and an extra blanket in a roll tied to the top of the pack. The gas mask is slung at the carry position on the left hip. Spiral wool puttees are worn in place of the peacetime canvas leggings. (4/19) NA

Left: These signalmen stand inspection with the M1911 .45 caliber pistol. The bolt has been drawn back to expose the empty chamber for the inspecting officer. The corporal in front has the crossed flags of the Signal Corps under his rank stripes. These branch of service markings on rank chevrons would disappear as the war progressed and everything was simplified. The armband around his left sleeve indicates he is either a messenger (if red) or a signalman (if blue). (1st Signal Field Bn. 5/18) NA

Bottom left: Wearing the shorter M1918 overcoat (without cuff straps), a member of the 317th engineers cleans his M1917 Enfield rifle in a German military cemetery. Although this rifle did not get as much publicity as the famous Springfield, the Enfield was used by approximately seventy-five per cent of Americans in the AEF. (92nd Div. 10/18) NA

Right: The 16-inch length of the M1905 bayonet is shown on a M1903 Springfield rifle. This was the most accurate rifle used by any country in the war. It carried five rounds in the magazine well, and continued to see service well into WW2. This man is credited with having killed a German with the butt of his rifle. He wears rubber hip boots commonly issued for deep mud or flooded trenches. (42nd Div. 5/18) NA

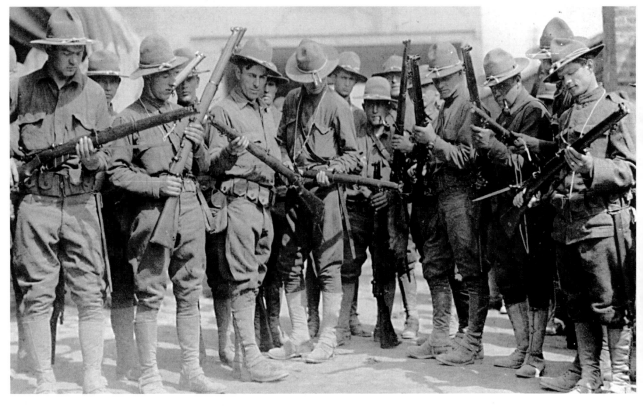

Above: These men from the Pennsylvania National Guard have exchanged their American rifles for British ones. Ammunition supply was simplified by issuing units attached to British or French Armies with weapons that took the same ammunition as used by the troops alongside whom they would fight. When transferred back to American control these men would once again receive U.S. weapons. (28th Div. 5/18) NA

Below: Telescopic sights were attached to the Springfield rifle for use by snipers. This rifle has been painted in a camouflage pattern to help conceal the sniper when he is hidden in no-man's-land. The sniper is wearing the two round dog tags on a fabric tape as directed by regulations. Note the regulation shirt which can only be unbuttoned halfway. (42nd Div. 5/18) NA

Right: The French 'VB' rifle grenade was adopted by the Americans, and grenade dischargers like this one were built for both the Springfield and Enfield rifles. The VB grenade had a central hole which allowed the bullet to pass right through it. The following gases were enough to propel the grenade 200 yards. Extra grenades were carried in the special pouch on the grenadier's left side. (6th Marines, 2nd Div. 9/18) NA

Above: The Americans did not have a good light machine gun design in 1917, so the French government supplied the Chauchat automatic rifle with twenty-round clips. The model designed for French ammunition worked well, but a modified Chauchat for American ammunition jammed frequently, which gave the weapon an unjustifiably poor reputation. Not until the 1980s was it discovered that the American versions had been made to the wrong specifications. (42nd Div. 7/18) NA

Right: The French Hotchkiss machine gun was used as a heavy machine gun by the first twelve American divisions to land in France. These were all replaced once enough M1917 Browning water-cooled machine guns were available. Ammunition was fed into the Hotchkiss with a straight 'feeder strip' of metal. (26th Div. 1/18) NA

Opposite page, top: At the very end of the war the Browning Automatic Rifle was supplied to the AEF to replace the Chauchat. This light weapon took a twenty-round box magazine, and was so successful that it was used by the U.S. Army through World War II and Korea. The BAR was only used in combat during the very last weeks of World War I. (83rd Div. 10/18) NA

Opposite page, top: The British Vickers machine gun was used by the 13th through 24th American Divisions sent to France. Water, in the distinctive fluted barrel jacket, boiled off as the heat of firing built up. The steam escaped down the rubber tube seen attached to the front of the barrel. The condensed water would then be recycled into the barrel jacket. This cooling system kept the gun from overheating and allowed for longer periods of firing. (77th Div. 5/18) NA

Opposite page, bottom: In a curious juxtaposition, a Hotchkiss machine gun is mounted on a horse-drawn wagon for defense against German airplanes. Much of the American Army still relied on horse-drawn wagons. These slow

columns were vulnerable to German aircraft which could cause great damage with machine guns and a few bombs. (6th F.A. 9/18) NA

Above: The M1917 Browning machine gun was the American replacement for the French Hotchkiss and British Vickers. At left Lieutenant V. Browning, son of the inventor, instructs men how to fire the weapon. Like the Vickers, the Browning was a water-cooled gun which could fire for a long period. Machine guns such as these often used the stability of their heavy tripod to fire at unseen targets well behind the German lines, much the same as artillery did. (80th Div. 10/18) NA

Left: The 37mm gun was a small artillery piece with a range of two miles that was used by the infantry on the front lines. It could be towed into position, then removed from the wheeled carriage for a lower (and more concealable) silhouette. There were three 37mm guns in an infantry regiment, each with a crew of eight men. (44th Regt, 8/18) NA

Left: The British-designed Stokes mortar shot an explosive round in a high arc, so it could be fired from inside one trench, over no-man's-land and right down into an enemy trench. Normal artillery came in at a low angle and caused little damage in the trenches unless a direct hit was made. Six of the 3-inch mortars (seen here) were in every infantry regiment, and another twelve of the 6-inch version were in the Artillery Brigade. (1st Corps, 8/18) NA

Below: The most famous artillery piece of the war was the rapid-firing French 75mm with a range of 5½ miles. Due to the advanced design of the recoil assembly the 75mm gun stayed on target after recoil, thus allowing for more rapidly aimed shots than the German equivalent. There were twenty-four French-supplied 75mm guns in every U.S. light artillery regiment (or forty-eight per division). (2nd Div. 7/18) NA

Bottom: The heaviest artillery piece in the division was the French Schneider 155mm howitzer. Every heavy artillery regiment had twenty-four of these guns (twenty-four per division). It had a range of seven miles. Some Schneiders were manufactured in the U.S., but none were ever shipped overseas. (32nd Div. 5/18) NA

Above: The Liberty Truck was a vehicle developed by the top American truck designers. It used the best designs of each truck company, and was made from standardized parts for ease of assembly and repair. Its cross-country ability is shown by the extreme position of the wheels in this rough terrain demonstration. (12/17) NA

Opposite page, top: Motorcycles proved a popular and speedy way to send messages. Here two motorcycles meet at a relay point to continue the delivery of important mail. When roads were in poor shape, the motorcycle could normally find a path to travel through the damaged area, or pass between stalled vehicles. (2nd Army Corps, 7/18) NA

Right: This truck is being given a camouflage paint scheme. A camouflage expert has outlined the different areas and indicated what color each of them should be. The painting was continued on to the canvas cover. Camouflage painting of vehicles was eliminated in June 1918 as not being effective. Note the M2 gas mask carried by the painter. (51st Coast Artillery, 5/18) NA

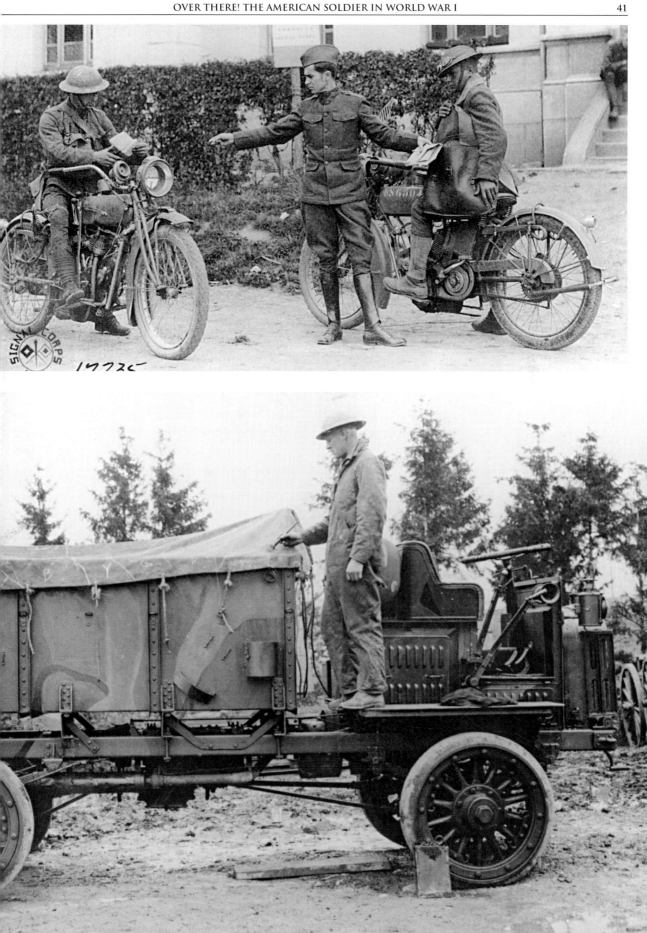

Above: Poison gas was also liable to affect the animals needed to haul supply wagons and artillery pieces. These mules wear one version of an equine gas mask. Other versions included goggles worn over the animal's eyes. Mules are not as sensitive to gas as humans, so the masks did not have to filter the air as thoroughly as a soldier's mask. (11/18) NA

Below: The eight steps to put on and adjust the standard gas mask are demonstrated from right to left. Inside the mask, the wearer breathes through a mouthpiece connected to the tube, while a clamp holds the nose shut. This gas mask was patterned after the British small box respirator. (83rd Div. 10/18) NA

Above: A squad of marines practice adjusting the French M2 gas mask. The M2 was essentially a mask of cloth impregnated with chemicals, and placed over the face. It was carried as a backup to the British-designed respirator, and was used for smoke, tear gas or weaker concentrations of poison gas. It was more comfortable and could be worn for longer periods than the small box respirator. (2nd Div. 1/18) NA

Below: Soldiers passing through a bath and disinfecting plant have gone through the showers, received new underclothing and are about to receive clean outer garments. Even though this area is probably far behind the lines, they still carry their M2 gas masks in the slung bag just in case there is a gas attack. (6/18) NA

Above: After a battle, American two-man tanks are being checked over and repaired for the next engagement. The different suits of cards painted on the tank were used to indicate different units. The Renault FT 17 tank was armed with a 37mm gun, and could travel at a speed of 6 mph. At the end of the war these tanks were being built in the U.S., but no American-built tanks took part in the fighting. (321st Tank Co. 10/18) NA

Left: The Renault tank had a crew of two men: one driver, and a commander/gunner who entered through the hatch seen on the rear of the turret. Leather jerkins, such as seen on this crew, were popular as they kept the men warm, but did not interfere with movement inside the cramped interior. The engine was so loud that the commander communicated with the driver by tapping with his foot on the back of the driver's head. (327th Tank Bn, 10/18) NA

Opposite page, bottom: The larger British tanks were manned by a crew of eight men and weighed 32 tons. American soldiers in Great Britain were trained in these 'heavy' tanks. Only one American-manned 'heavy' tank battalion saw combat, as part of the British Army, at the very end of the war. Here a British-operated tank is shown in training with the American 27th Division. The Americans have been armed with the British model Enfield rifle because they have been temporarily attached to the British Army. (27th Div. 9/18) NA

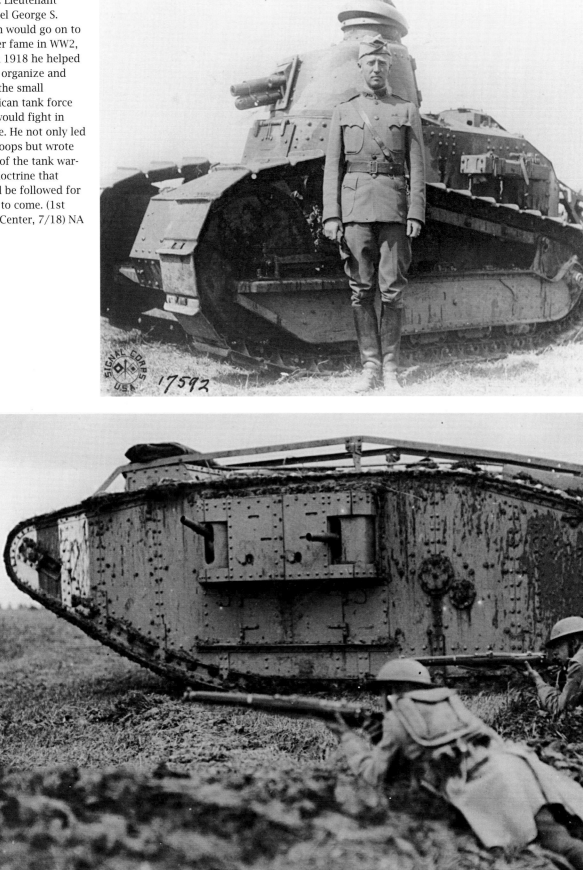

Right: Lieutenant Colonel George S. Patton would go on to greater fame in WW2, but in 1918 he helped form, organize and train the small American tank force that would fight in France. He not only led the troops but wrote most of the tank warfare doctrine that would be followed for years to come. (1st Tank Center, 7/18) NA

Left: From left to right: Lieutenant Eddie Rickenbacker (America's greatest air ace), Lieutenant Douglas Campbell (the first American ace), and Captain Kenneth Marr. They illustrate both the closed and open collar tunics worn by aviation officers. At the start of the war aeroplanes were under the jurisdiction of the Signal Corps, so they display the corps insignia on their uniforms. They all wear the British-version two-buttoned overseas cap. No American-built aeroplane ever fought in combat in the war, only French or British planes with American crews. (94th Aero Sqdn. 6/18) NA

Below: An important aspect of aviation was the use of balloons as observation platforms. Observers could accurately direct artillery to specific targets from these baskets, which were connected to the ground by a telephone. Once airborne, this two-man crew will become a prime target for German aeroplanes, enemy machine guns and artillery. (4/18) NA

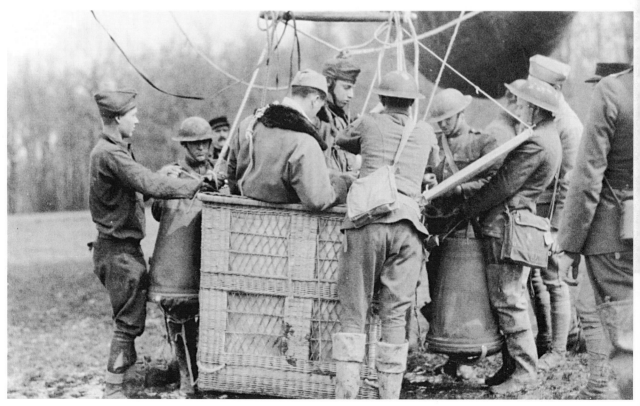

Above: An aeroplane crew prepares to take off on a reconnaissance mission. The pilot (standing) wears a warm coat to protect against the severe cold found at high altitudes. The observer rides in the rear seat and will alternate between taking reconnaissance photos and manning the Lewis machine gun to defend against German attacks. (88th Aero Sqdn.) NA

Above: The air war was not all glamor and fancy uniforms. Aviators such as Lieutenant Henry MacLure had to put up with cold, wet and muddy airfields. He wears woolen puttees and a warm trenchcoat – something he would be glad to have when his plane was later forced down over German lines. Unable to avoid being captured, he spent the rest of the war in a POW camp, although the Germans did present him with a photograph of his downed aircraft. (139th Aero Sdrn) HM

Left: Major Holland Smith is most famous for his command of U.S. Marines in the Pacific fighting of WW2. In 1918 he was a marine officer serving in France. He wears the officer's forest-green wool uniform, with the eagle, globe and anchor device on his collar. (3/18) NA

Opposite page, top: A navy corpsman provides first aid to a marine while on a training hike. The marines do not have their own medical personnel, so they borrow them from the Navy. Visible on the medic's left arm is a Maltese Cross indicating a corpsman. The marine corporal appears to wear a campaign hat with the brim cut off. Note that no collar disks are worn on the marine green tunic. (2nd Div. 2/18) NA

Opposite page, bottom: A marine unit with full pack is preparing to leave for the front lines. They wear the forest-green marine uniform. In order to make supply easier, and not confuse the marine green with the German field gray, the marines were ordered to trade in their uniforms for the army olive drab uniform. Once the change to olive drab was made, the marines added USMC collar disks so as not to be mistaken for army troops. (5th Marines, 5/18) NA

Below: French Alpine troops with their distinctive berets were used as instructors for the first American units landing in France. Here they watch a demonstration of M1911 pistol marksmanship by a marine. For an unknown reason he wears a cavalry holster that swivels at the top. Marines originally wore the eagle, globe and anchor insignia on their campaign hats. They later wore it on the front of their steel helmets. (2nd Div. 1917) NA

Opposite page, top: The American Red Cross performed many different humanitarian services during the war. To take some of the strain off the U.S. government, the Red Cross agreed to provide morale-building services, such as this canteen, to the AEF. Here a Red Cross worker serves a drink to a doughboy wearing the full pack and rubber boots. He is probably on his way back to the trenches. (42nd Div. 11/18) NA

Opposite page, bottom: The Salvation Army was another of the many organizations that provided services to the troops. They are best known for what is seen here: making dough-nuts. Even though they are non-combatants in the rear area, gas masks hang close by on the tent pole. NA

Below: The 'Hello Girls' were a group of French-speaking American telephone operators who provided valuable communications and translation skills to the AEF. Many replaced their wide-brimmed hats with overseas caps of the same style as the army. They wear armbands embroidered with the insignia of the Signal Corps to indicate their official status. Their long skirts would have small lead weights in the hem to prevent wind from immodestly blowing their skirts up. (5/18) NA

Above: Men of the 369th Regiment (formerly the 15th New York) display their American uniforms and their French equipment. Helmets, gas masks, ammo pouches, belts and weapons have all been supplied by the French Army. The Americans were unsure if the Negro troops would fight, but the French welcomed them into the front lines and allowed this unit to prove its fighting ability. (93rd Div.) NA

Below: This view of the 369th Regiment in the trenches clearly shows the French weapons carried by these men. The first four men are armed with three French Lebel rifles, and a Chauchat machine gun. The first soldier has a VB grenade discharger on his rifle. The white officer behind them wears the French helmet as well, but an American pistol belt. (369th Regt. 5/18) NA

Right: This ship is returning wounded men to the States. In the front row one man wears the patch of the 93rd Division: a blue French helmet on a black circle. This signified their use of French equipment. Behind him a man wears a French-made overseas cap with the regimental numbers of the 372nd Regiment. Placing the numbers on the hat was a French habit picked up by this unit, and not authorized in the U.S. Army. He also wears the French Croix de Guerre medal. (93rd Div.) NA

Above: These soldiers were used for moving supplies behind the combat area. They have continued to wear the campaign hat, as their unit would not be sent into combat and thus need the steel helmet. Of great interest is the man just to the right of the banjo. He wears a poorly fitted British Army tunic (indicated by the collar and pleated pockets). Negro units like this frequently received the poorest of uniforms in the supply system. (301st Stevedore Regt, 5/18) NA

Opposite page, top: There was a joke that the war would last one hundred years: five years for fighting, and ninety-five years for rolling up the barbed wire. This group of engineers is being instructed in placing barbed wire. The metal pickets could be screwed into the ground, which was quieter than hammering in stakes. A strand of barbed wire could be run through the looped eyes quickly and easily in the dark. (41st Div. 8/18) NA

Below left: The majority of troop movements were made by men marching over endless roads. A periodic foot inspection was needed to check on the condition of the men's feet. This became particularly important in the winter when trench foot, caused by standing in cold, wet trenches, resulted in a great many casualties. Trench foot could be prevented by frequent changes to dry socks. (83rd Div. 10/18) NA

Right: Battalion Sergeant Major Sherman Ford of the 32nd Division headquarters wears his rank insignia on only one sleeve, as per regulations. Even such small items as these were in short supply due to the scarcity of shipping space. In addition to his two dog tags, he wears an identity bracelet on his wrist to make sure that his body could be identified. The two diagonal stripes on his sleeves are for officer candidates at one of the AEF schools. He has tied his puttees at the bottom in the style of mounted troops (infantry tied them at the top). (32nd Div. 1/19)

Opposite page, top: Men of the 18th Machine Gun Battalion sit in front of their pup tents repairing uniforms and searching for lice. Body lice, commonly called 'cooties', was a major problem in all armies. The constant irritation of lice kept men from sleeping, and caused general misery. Lice also posed a serious risk of transmitting diseases such as typhus. Soldiers kept their hair very short to prevent lice from infesting it. (1st Div. 5/18) NA

Opposite page, bottom: To combat the spread of lice, men returning from the trenches would have their uniforms sent through a delousing machine. Extreme heat and steam would kill all lice and their eggs living in the seams of the uniforms. This treatment shrunk the vegetable ivory buttons used on many uniforms, which stressed the supply system even further to replace them with metal ones. (1st Div. 5/18) NA

Above: After the soldiers had passed through showers and had their uniforms disinfected they were issued with replacement items. In the harsh combat environment, uniforms were ripped to shreds on barbed wire, shattered trees and rural debris. Soldiers were constantly in need of new clothing, and much of it was supplied by French and British manufacturers. (6/18) NA

Left: The French railway carriages were marked with the legend '40 men or 8 horses', which gave rise to their nickname of 'forty and eights'. After the war a veterans' association used the same name to refer to their members who had served in the AEF. Two quartermaster officers in short overcoats supervise the unloading of hay for their unit's horses. (2nd Div. 10/18) NA

Opposite page, bottom: Every man carried one shelter half, which was half of a pup-tent. In cold weather the overcoat was used to cover up the front opening. At the far right of this inspection display can be seen a French Chauchat magazine bag. Just in front of the tent pole are eight cardboard boxes of hard bread ration. (42nd Div. 6/18) NA

Below: Corrugated iron allowed for rapid construction of shelter. This half piece could be placed over a hole and covered with earth to provide instant protection. Two such pieces could be bolted together to form a larger shelter. Although the thin metal was no protection from heavy artillery, it did protect the men from small pieces of flying metal, stones and clumps of earth. (42nd Div. 5/18) NA

Opposite page, top: Soldiers in the trenches often had a hard time getting food delivered to them through enemy shellfire. These men share a meal, possibly still hot, brought up in an insulated Marmite can. Clearly visible at far right is the leather tab on the British-produced small box respirator. The American version of this mask had an all-metal attachment. (26th Div. 5/18) NA

Above: The YMCA ran many canteens through France to help keep up the morale of the enlisted men. Here they could write letters home, play games, drink coffee and generally relax. The sale of alcohol to any man in uniform was prohibited by the U.S. Army, but the troops could always find some intoxicating beverage for sale in a local French town. (26th Div. 4/18) NA

Left: A typical chow line set up in the rear feeds men waiting patiently with mess kits and canteen cups. The standard meal provided to the AEF was called 'slum', a varied concoction related to stew. It contained whatever ingredients the cooks happened to have on hand, as well as left-overs from previous meals. (12/18) NA

Left: Many different methods of communication were used by the Army. The most interesting were the carrier pigeons that were brought into the thick of battle. A message was tied to their legs and then the birds were released to fly back to their perches at headquarters. Although crude by today's standards, the pigeons were frequently more reliable than the early radios or telephones. (2nd Corps, 10/18) NA

Below: The use of field telephones allowed for better communications, but the wires were frequently cut by enemy shellfire. This operator runs a small switchboard connecting a number of different lines. The early telephones employed only a single wire with the earth as the ground (or return). This meant that the enemy could use special equipment to listen in on phone conversations. (11/15) NA

Working from a map, this officer could be either directing artillery barrages or ordering up troops. Both he and his aide wear their gas mask bags in the proper fashion with the flap next to their bodies. This prevented any mud from getting into the bag if they had to crawl along the ground. Note the officer's leather leggings, instead of wool puttees, worn over short boots. NA

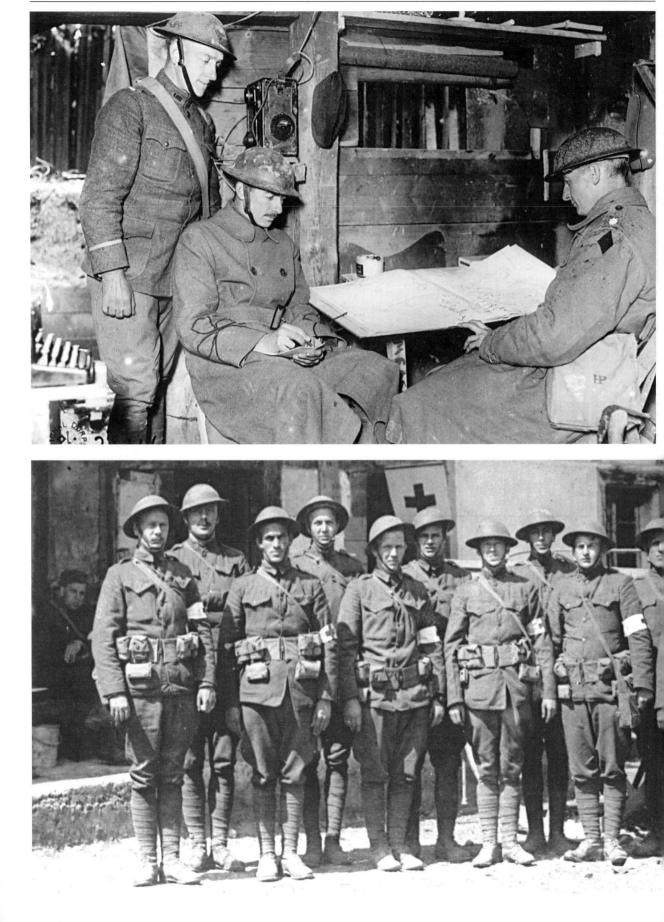

Opposite page, top: These officers study a map while in the safety of their dugout. The central figure wears the regulation officer's overcoat with the single strand of cuff braid for a lieutenant. At the right, the lieutenant colonel wears a 5th Division insignia on the left sleeve of his trenchcoat. The letters 'HP' on his gas mask bag are his initials. On the lieutenant at left can be seen the ring of braid worn around the cuff of all officers' tunics. (5th Div. 10/18) NA

Above: This advanced dressing station was constructed out of two corrugated metal sections. If the men stayed in this area for any length of time, they would begin to cover it with earth for greater protection. The medics, with Red Cross armbands, wear the leather helmet strap behind their necks. If an artillery shell landed near them, the concussion would then merely blow off the helmets instead of snapping their necks. (79th Div. 11/18) NA

Left: This sanitary (or medical) detachment served the 121st Machine Gun Battalion. The medics wear the enlisted man's medical belt with ten large pockets to hold bandages. On the front of the belts hang two smaller pouches. One was for the medic's personal bandage if he was wounded. The other, slightly larger, held tags to mark where and when the casualties were found, as well as any treatment applied. (32nd Div. 6/18) NA

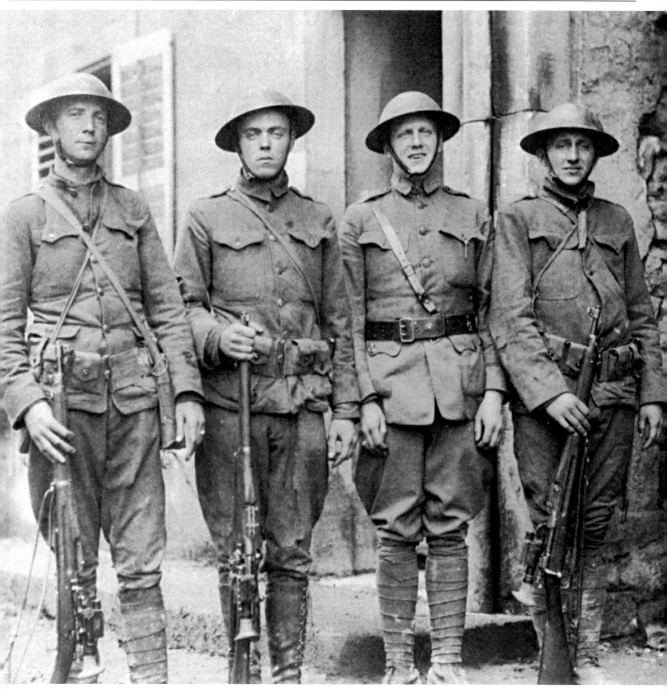

Opposite page, top: Trench raids were thought to have been originated by Canadian troops, but all nations were conducting them by the end of the war. A party of men would quietly slip across no-man's-land to capture enemy prisoners for interrogation. Raids that captured even one prisoner were considered successful. When the German lines were broken at the end of the war, large numbers of prisoners, such as those seen here, were taken. (32nd Div. 10/18) NA

Opposite page, bottom: This trench-raiding party from the 166th Regiment is composed of two men with pistols, two riflemen (both with pistols as well) and one Chauchat. They have stripped down to comfortable clothing, but all retain their lightweight M2 gas mask. Note the branch of service braid on the officer's overseas cap. (42nd Div. 5/18) NA

Above: Although captioned as a trench-raiding party, all three enlisted men carry rifles with telescopic sights. This may indicate that the men went out into no-man's-land to set up sniper positions to observe and shoot at the German lines when morning came. There was frequently so much debris between the trenches that men could conceal themselves very well. (42nd Div. 5/18) NA

Above: Marching to the front lines could seem endless. Every hour a ten-minute break would be taken to allow men to rest. Most troops considered it a matter of pride to stay with their unit and not fall out to the side of the road. In the foreground can be seen spare boots strapped to a pack. In theory, the men were to alternate their two pairs of boots every other day. (1st Div. 3/18) NA

Right: The U.S. Navy contributed the largest guns on the Western Front. The eight 14-inch railway guns had a range of over 45,000 yards. They arrived at the front in September 1918, and quickly were able to destroy the vital German railway lines running up and down the front. This eliminated the Germans' ability to move reserve troops and supplies, and may have contributed to the end of the war more than anyone has admitted. (10/18) NA

Opposite page, top: As the Americans gained ground and captured German trenches, they enjoyed the fruits of their victory. Here artillery officers sample the beer left behind in a German canteen. Note the different styles of privately purchased 'trench boots' worn by the officers. One man wears two service chevrons on his left sleeve, indicating twelve months' overseas service. (3rd Div.9/18) NA

22503

Left: A little known aspect of the war was the single unit the Americans sent to Italy to help bolster the Italian defense against the Austrian Army. The 332nd Infantry Regiment was dispatched to Italy in July 1918 where it fought at Vittoria Veneto. The Italians were good fighters and held their mountain lines against the Austrian Army for years. Their morale crumbled when confronted with well-trained German assault troops who became available due to the collapse of the Russian Army on the Eastern Front. (332nd Regt. 10/18) NA

Below: The platoon was the basic combat unit and was organized on the same lines as the British and French platoons. The fifty-nine-man unit had a six-man headquarters and four sections: a twelve-man hand grenade section with rifles and pistols, a nine-man rifle grenade section with six grenade dischargers, a seventeen-man rifle section and a fifteen-man automatic rifle section with two Chauchat teams. In this photo the Chauchat has been replaced by the BAR. (1st Div. 4/19) NA

Below: The presence of the 332nd American Infantry Regiment was instrumental in rebuilding the morale of the Italian soldier, as he realized that his country was not alone in the war. To make the 332nd look like a larger unit, the individual battalions were marched down different roads in the day, then recalled at night. The following day they would march a different path to make it seem that there were more Americans in Italy than was the case. This was done both to impress the friendly Italians and deceive enemy spies. (332nd Regt. 11/18) NA

Opposite page, top: After the Armistice of 11 November, elements of the Allied armies moved in to occupy sections of Germany. The U.S. Third Army became the U.S. 'Army of Occupation', as indicated by their shoulder patch of an 'A' inside an 'O'. The army served in the area around Koblenz until 1923. This medic with enlisted man's medical belt is providing care at one of many field exercises held to keep the men battle-ready. (3rd Army, 1921) NA

Opposite page, bottom: One of the main jobs of the Army after the war was taking care of wounded and disabled servicemen. At this U.S. military hospital a drill competition between one-legged men serves as a means to increase their ability to function. The U.S. Army suffered 323,000 casualties, but this pales in comparison with the 3,000,000 British, 6,000,000 French, 7,000,000 Germans, and an estimated 9,000,000 Russians wounded and killed. GG

Below: Unsatisfied with the British-style flat helmet, the Americans attempted to develop a better design. The soldier with the 'Liberty Bell' helmet is seen here on the left in mock combat with a man in a German helmet and gas mask. Similarity to the German helmet, plus the end of the war, prevented this design from being accepted, although Switzerland adopted a nearly identical model for its own army. (11/18) NA

Above: The Composite Regiment was composed of the best soldiers from the Army of Occupation. They were employed as escorts for dignitaries and in parades such as the main victory parade in Paris. These men were fiercely proud of being chosen for this elite unit, and frequently added a small letter 'c' to their shoulder patch to indicate their status. (1919) NA

Left: A new uniform for American troops was designed at the end of the war. It combined the best aspects of all Allied uniforms. The regimental numbers were displayed (French-style) in cloth letters on collars and cap. Breeches gave way to British-style trousers. The vast quantities of U.S. uniforms already stockpiled made it economically impossible to implement this new design, and American troops would continue to wear the same uniform until 1926. (12/18) NA

Right: The baseball team of the American members of the Paris Peace Commission wear the 'scales of liberty' armband to indicate they are part of that organization. Although the Armistice was signed in November 1918, the actual treaty ending the war was not signed until 28 June 1919. NA

Below: An American soldier (at right) stands guard in an M1918 overcoat, rubber overshoes and the M1907 winter hat. He guards the Trans-Siberian railway alongside a Japanese soldier. Over 10,000 Americans served in a multi-national force guarding Siberian ports, supply dumps and railways until January 1920. (11/18) NA

Above: Men of the 339th Infantry Regiment return to their camp after a week of fighting the Bolsheviks in northern Russia. They were sent to protect the ports, ensure that supplies sent to the Russian Army to fight the Germans did not fall into the hands of the Communist revolutionaries, and to help evacuate the Czech Army trapped in Russia. The only special cold-weather uniform they wear are leather jerkins, mittens and fur caps. (85th Div. 4/19) NA

Left: American troops fire a British Vickers machine while training in Archangel in northern Russia. Officers of the British Machine Gun Corps stand behind, observing the crew. The heavy overcoats and fur caps are British Army issue, and were needed as the temperature frequently dropped below zero. (85th Div. 1/19) NA

Above: In the warmer months members of the North Russian Expeditionary Force were relatively comfortable in their regular uniforms. These men from the 339th Regiment stand in front of their headquarters. The lonely feeling of being forgotten, at what seemed to be the end of the world, was especially acute as winter set in and it became increasingly difficult to obtain supplies from home. (85th Div. 9/18). NA

Below: The international nature of the NREF is indicated by these men of the 339th Regiment preparing to be awarded the French Croix de Guerre by the force commander who is a British general. The men carry the Russian model Mosin-Nagant rifle, for which ammunition supplies were plentiful. (85th Div. 2/19) NA

Above: A few U.S. Army units saw service in China until 1938. Here Company E of the 31st Infantry Regiment marches through a Chinese city to 'show the flag'. The company guidon appears to be reversed as it can only be properly read from the other side. The first man in line wears the three-pocket BAR magazine bandolier across his chest. NA

Left: The M1926 officer's uniform is worn here by cavalryman Captain Hugh Fitzgerald. He wears breeches of a lighter shade, as was the habit picked up from the British Army in World War I. By the 1930s every major unit had its own shoulder insignia, with many smaller units having an enamelled crest (visible here in the center of the captain's shoulder straps). (3rd Cavalry Regt. 1932) NA

Right: Signalmen in the 1930s lay telephone wire from reels on the back of their Chevrolet truck. They wear the M1926 open collar tunic with shirt and tie. In winter the wool breeches were worn, while the cotton ones were for summer use. The service cap was generally worn for dress, while the older campaign hat was still used for the field. The wool puttees continued to be worn for field exercises, while canvas and leather leggings were kept for garrison use. A brown leather garrison belt is worn with the tunic. (1st Inf. Div. Special Troops) NA

Right: The U.S. Army had garrisoned the Philippine Islands since they were captured from the Spanish in 1898. This lieutenant wears a khaki cotton shirt and breeches while serving as the Provost Marshal (note the PM armband). He is shown greeting King Alphonso of Negritos. The custom of wearing a shirt as an outer garment started in Panama, then spread to all hot climates. (1931) NA

'Rags', the mascot of the 1st Division, wears two wound stripes on his uniform. His caretaker illustrates some insignia that developed in and after World War I. The first sergeant wears a single wound stripe on his right sleeve and four service chevrons on his left, indicating two years overseas duty in World War I. Also on his left are four diagonal 'hash marks' indicating four periods of enlistment. The striped cord around his left shoulder is the French Fourragère awarded to his unit in World War I. The divisional insignia of the 1st Division is on the left shoulder, and the regimental crests (the 16th Infantry Regiment) are on the collar just above the collar disks. On the WW1 victory medal are five clasps indicating five different wartime engagements. NA

INDEX